To:

_____

From:

_____

Date:

_____

© 2010 Summerside Press™
Minneapolis 55438
www.summersidepress.com

Proverbs

A *Pocket Inspirations* Book

ISBN 978-1-935416-90-6

Scripture references are from the following sources: The Holy Bible, New International Version® NIV®. © 1973, 1978, 1984 by Biblica, Inc.™ Used by permission of Zondervan. The New King James Version (NKJV). Copyright © 1982 by Thomas Nelson, Inc. Used by permission. The Holy Bible, New Living Translation® (NLT). Copyright © 1996, 2004. Used by permission of Tyndale House Publishers, Inc., Wheaton, Illinois 60189. The Holy Bible, English Standard Version® (ESV), copyright © 2001 by Crossway Bibles, a publishing ministry of Good News Publishers. Used by permission. All rights reserved. *The Message* (MSG) © 1993, 1994, 1995, 1996, 2000, 2001, 2002 by Eugene Peterson. Used by permission of NavPress, Colorado Springs, CO. All rights reserved. The New Century Version® (NCV). Copyright © 1987, 1988, 1991, 2005 by Thomas Nelson Inc. Used by permission. All rights reserved.

Compiled by Marilyn Jansen
Designed by Lisa & Jeff Franke

Summerside Press™ is an inspirational publisher offering fresh, irresistible books to uplift the heart and engage the mind.

Printed in USA.

Proverbs

A *Pocket Inspirations* Book

Pi Pocket
INSPIRATIONS

summerside
PRESS

The Tablet of Your Heart

Let love and faithfulness never leave you; bind them around your neck, write them on the tablet of your heart. Then you will win favor and a good name in the sight of God and man. Trust in the LORD with all your heart and lean not on your own understanding; in all your ways acknowledge him, and he will make your paths straight.

PROVERBS 3:3–6 NIV

The road to the head lies through the heart.

AMERICAN PROVERB

Those who are steadily learning how to love are
enabled to do this because the very love of God,
Himself, has been put into our hearts.

EUGENIA PRICE

Good sense is a fountain of life to him who has it,
but the instruction of fools is folly.

PROVERBS 16:22 ESV

The head learns new things, but the heart
forevermore practices old experiences.

HENRY WARD BEECHER

The riches that are in the heart cannot be stolen.

RUSSIAN PROVERB

Commonsense Faith

True friendship with God...means being so
intimately in touch with God that you never
even need to ask Him to show you His will.
You are God's will. And all of your seemingly
commonsense decisions are actually His will for
you, unless you sense a check in your spirit.

OSWALD CHAMBERS

Dear friend, guard Clear Thinking and Common
Sense with your life; don't for a minute lose sight
of them. They'll keep your soul alive and well,
they'll keep you fit and attractive.

PROVERBS 3:21–22 MSG

Act quickly, think slowly.

GREEK PROVERB

Faith declares what the senses do not see,
but not the contrary of what they see.
It is above them, not contrary to them.

BLAISE PASCAL

Don't turn your back on wisdom,
for she will protect you.
Love her, and she will guard you.
Getting wisdom is the wisest thing you can do!
And whatever else you do, develop good judgment.

PROVERBS 4:6–7 NLT

Teachers point to the door,
but you must enter by yourself.

CHINESE PROVERB

A Bright Start

We can get a right start only by accepting
God as He is and learning to love Him
for what He is. As we go on to know
Him better we shall find it a source
of unspeakable joy that God is just what He is.

A. W. TOZER

False weights and unequal measures—
the Lord detests double standards of every kind.
Even children are known by the way they act,
whether their conduct is pure,
and whether it is right.

PROVERBS 20:10–11 NLT

Wise is he who can take the little moment
as it comes and make it brighter ere 'tis gone.

DANIEL ORCUTT

The ways of right-living people glow with
light; the longer they live, the brighter they
shine. But the road of wrongdoing gets
darker and darker—travelers can't see a
thing; they fall flat on their faces.

PROVERBS 4:18 MSG

God's promises are like the stars; the darker
the night the brighter they shine.

DAVID NICHOLAS

Only the still pool reflects the stars.

CHINESE PROVERB

Speak Carefully

For attractive lips,
Speak words of kindness.

SAM LEVENSON

Kind words are like honey—
sweet to the soul
and healthy for the body.

PROVERBS 16:24 NLT

Sometimes it is necessary for us to speak.
At other times it is important that we be quiet.
Wisdom comes with knowing the difference.

MRS. D. E. CLAY

Actions are fruits; words are but leaves.

ENGLISH PROVERB

Gold there is, and rubies in abundance, but lips that speak knowledge are a rare jewel.

PROVERBS 20:15 NIV

Talking comes by nature, silence by wisdom.

AMERICAN PROVERB

Whoever keeps his mouth and his tongue keeps himself out of trouble.

PROVERBS 21:23 ESV

The Making of a Life

The LORD brought me forth as the first of his works, before his deeds of old; I was appointed from eternity, from the beginning, before the world began. When there were no oceans, I was given birth, when there were no springs abounding with water; before the mountains were settled in place, before the hills, I was given birth, before he made the earth or its fields or any of the dust of the world.

PROVERBS 8:22–26 NIV

The wise don't expect to find life worth living; they make it that way.

From what we get, we can make a living;
what we give, however, makes a life.

ARTHUR ASHE

It pays to take life seriously;
things work out when you trust in God.
A wise person gets known for insight;
gracious words add to one's reputation.

PROVERBS 16:20–21 MSG

If you would be happy all your life,
plant a garden.

CHINESE PROVERB

Friends Stick Together

Friends are an indispensable part of a meaningful life. They are the ones who share our burdens and multiply our blessings. A true friend sticks by us in our joys and sorrows. In good times and bad, we need friends who will pray for us, listen to us, and lend a comforting hand and an understanding ear when needed.

BEVERLY LaHaye

Bring bread to the table and your friends will bring their joy to share.

FRENCH PROVERB

There are "friends" who destroy each other,
but a real friend sticks closer than a brother.

PROVERBS 18:24 NLT

A friend is somebody who loves us with
understanding, as well as emotion.

ROBERT LOUIS STEVENSON

An open rebuke
is better than hidden love!
Wounds from a sincere friend
are better than many kisses from an enemy.

PROVERBS 27:5–6 NLT

Hold a true friend with both your hands.

NIGERIAN PROVERB

Trust God's Process

Listen to my instruction and be wise;
do not ignore it.
Blessed is the man who listens to me,
watching daily at my doors,
waiting at my doorway.
For whoever finds me finds life
and receives favor from the LORD.

PROVERBS 8:33–35 NIV

God is here. I have joyously discovered
that He is always "up to something" in my life,
and I am learning to quit second-guessing
Him and simply trust the process.

GLORIA GAITHER

Things never go so well that one
should have no fear, and never
so ill that one should have no hope.

TURKISH PROVERB

*The teaching of the wise is a fountain
of life, that one may turn away
from the snares of death.*

PROVERBS 13:14 ESV

You can never change the past. But by the
grace of God, you can win the future.
So remember those things which will help
you forward, but forget those things which
will only hold you back.

RICHARD C. WOODSOME

He Is the Source

The implications of the name *Immanuel*
are comforting.... Comforting, because He has
come to share the danger as well as the drudgery
of our everyday lives. He desires to weep with
us and to wipe away our tears. And what seems
most bizarre, Jesus Christ, the Son of God,
longs to share in and to be the source of the
laughter and the joy we all too rarely know.

MICHAEL CARD

Charm is deceptive, and beauty is fleeting; but
a woman who fears the LORD is to be praised.
Give her the reward she has earned, and let her
works bring her praise at the city gate.

PROVERBS 31:30–31 NIV

He is the Source. Of everything. Strength for
your day. Wisdom for your task. Comfort for
your soul. Grace for your battle. Provision for
each need. Understanding for each failure.
Assistance for every encounter.

JACK HAYFORD

Wisdom is found on the lips of the discerning....
Wise men store up knowledge,
but the mouth of a fool invites ruin.

PROVERBS 10:13–14 NIV

Give thanks for unknown blessings
already on their way.

NATIVE AMERICAN PROVERB

Safe in God

We do not understand the intricate
pattern of the stars in their courses, but
we know that He who created them does,
and that just as surely as He guides them,
He is charting a safe course for us.

BILLY GRAHAM

Have no fear of sudden disaster or of the
ruin that overtakes the wicked, for the
LORD will be your confidence and will
keep your foot from being snared.

PROVERBS 3:25–26 NIV

God's help is nearer than the door.

IRISH PROVERB

*People with integrity walk safely,
but those who follow crooked paths
will slip and fall.
People who wink at wrong cause trouble,
but a bold reproof promotes peace.*

PROVERBS 10:9–10 NLT

When we are told that God, who is our
dwelling place, is also our fortress, it can only
mean one thing, and that is that if we will
but live in our dwelling place, we shall be
perfectly safe and secure from every assault of
every possible enemy that can attack us.

HANNAH WHITALL SMITH

The Wisdom of Advice

Pride only breeds quarrels, but wisdom
is found in those who take advice.

PROVERBS 13:10 NIV

A true friend...advises justly,
assists readily, adventures boldly,
takes all patiently, defends courageously,
and continues a friend unchangeably.

WILLIAM PENN

Without wise leadership, a nation falls;
there is safety in having many advisers.

PROVERBS 11:14 NLT

In giving advice, seek to help,
not please, your friend.

SOLON

Many receive advice;
only the wise profit from it.

PUBLILIUS SYRUS

The right word at the right time is like a
custom-made piece of jewelry, and a wise
friend's timely reprimand is like a gold ring
slipped on your finger.

PROVERBS 25:11–12 MSG

A single conversation across the table with a
wise man is worth a month's study of books.

CHINESE PROVERB

The best way to succeed in life is to act
on the advice we give others.

A Wise Life

He who walks with the wise grows wise,
but a companion of fools suffers harm.

PROVERBS 13:20 NIV

Wise people, even though all laws were
abolished, would still lead the same life.

ARISTOPHANES

I, wisdom, dwell together with prudence;
I possess knowledge and discretion.
To fear the LORD is to hate evil;
I hate pride and arrogance,
evil behavior and perverse speech.
Counsel and sound judgment are mine;
I have understanding and power.

PROVERBS 8:12–14 NIV

If only man could get a little older a little later,
and a little wiser a little younger.

DICK GREGORY

What I have kept I have lost;
what I spent I had, what I gave I have.

PERSIAN PROVERB

The wise have wealth and luxury,
but fools spend whatever they get.
Whoever pursues righteousness and unfailing love
will find life, righteousness, and honor.
The wise conquer the city of the strong
and level the fortress in which they trust.

PROVERBS 21:20–22 NLT

I hear, and I forget. I see, and I remember.
I do, and I understand.

CHINESE PROVERB

Joy and Happiness

There is joy in heaven when a tear of sorrow is
shed in the presence of a truly understanding
heart. And heaven will never forget that joy.

CHARLES MALIK

The prospect of the righteous is joy,
but the hopes of the wicked come to nothing.

PROVERBS 10:28 NIV

A part of our petition must always be
for an increasing discernment so that we
can see things as God sees them. We may ask
for greater faith so that we can heal others,
but God, who understands human need far
better than we do, gives us greater compassion
so that we can weep with others.

RICHARD J. FOSTER

If you desire to be really happy,
you must make God
your final and ultimate goal.

THOMAS À KEMPIS

Now, my children, listen to me,
because those who follow my ways are happy.

PROVERBS 8:32 NCV

Unshared joy is an unlighted candle.

SPANISH PROVERB

A merry heart makes a cheerful countenance,
But by sorrow of the heart the spirit is broken.

PROVERBS 15:13 NKJV

The Way of Wisdom

I guide you in the way of wisdom and lead
you along straight paths. When you walk,
your steps will not be hampered; when you
run, you will not stumble.

PROVERBS 4:11–12 NIV

God give me joy in the common things:
In the dawn that lures, the eve that sings....
In the songs of children, unrestrained;
In the sober wisdom age has gained.
God give me joy in the tasks that press,
In the memories that burn and bless;
In the thought that life has love to spend,
In the faith that God's at journey's end.
God give me hope for each day that springs,
God give me joy in the common things!

THOMAS CURTIS CLARK

Life is so generous a giver,
but we, judging its gifts
by the covering,
cast them away as ugly,
or heavy or hard.
Remove the covering
and you will find beneath it
a living splendor,
woven of love,
by wisdom, with power.

FRÀ GIOVANNI GIOCONDO

Let the wise hear and increase in learning,
and the one who understands obtain guidance,
to understand a proverb and a saying,
the words of the wise and their riddles.

PROVERBS 1:5–6 ESV

Eternal Dignity

She is clothed with strength and dignity; she
can laugh at the days to come. She speaks with
wisdom, and faithful instruction is on her tongue.

PROVERBS 31:25–26 NIV

You ought to trust me for I do not
love and will never love
any woman in the world but you,
and my chief desire is to link
myself to you week by week by bonds
which shall ever become
more intimate and profound.
Beloved, I kiss your memory—
your sweetness and beauty have cast
a glory upon my life.

WINSTON CHURCHILL
(in a letter to his wife, Clementine)

Who can find a virtuous and capable wife?
She is more precious than rubies.
Her husband can trust her,
and she will greatly enrich his life.
She brings him good, not harm,
all the days of her life.

PROVERBS 31:10–12 NLT

Our love is like the misty rain that
falls softly—but floods the river.

AFRICAN PROVERB

Love prospers when a fault is forgiven,
but dwelling on it separates close friends.

PROVERBS 17:9 NLT

The Blessing of Friends

Don't praise yourself. Let someone else do it.
Let the praise come from a stranger
and not from your own mouth.

PROVERBS 27:2 NCV

I account that one of the greatest
demonstrations of real friendship is that a
friend can really endeavor to have his friend
advanced in honor, in reputation, in the
opinion of wit or learning, before himself.

JEREMY TAYLOR

Perfume and incense bring joy to the heart,
and the pleasantness of one's friend springs
from his earnest counsel.

PROVERBS 27:9 NIV

What a blessing is a friend with a heart
so trustworthy that you may safely bury all
your secrets in it, whose conscience you may
fear less than your own, who can relieve your
cares by his words, your doubts by his advice,
your sadness by his good humor, and whose
very look gives comfort to you.

A friend loves at all times,
And a brother is born for adversity.

PROVERBS 17:17 NKJV

Who is more indefatigable in toil,
when there is occasion for toil, than a friend?
Who is readier to rejoice in one's good
fortune? Whose praise is sweeter? From whose
lips does one learn the truth with less pain?
What fortress, what bulwarks, what arms
are more steadfast than loyal hearts?

JOHN CHRYSOSTOM

Loving Instruction

It behooves a father to be blameless if he expects
his son to be more blameless than he was himself.

TITUS MACCIUS PLAUTUS

The purposes of a man's heart are deep waters,
but a man of understanding draws them out.
Many a man claims to have unfailing love,
but a faithful man who can find?
The righteous man leads a blameless life;
blessed are his children after him.

PROVERBS 20:5–7 NIV

If you have a habit of being attentive and
expressing interest, your children will not confuse
your loving instruction with rejection.

CHARLES STANLEY

A fool despises his father's instruction,
But he who receives correction is prudent.
In the house of the righteous there
is much treasure,
But in the revenue of the wicked is trouble.

PROVERBS 15:5–6 NKJV

Neither let mistakes nor wrong directions,
of which every man, in his studies and elsewhere,
falls into many, discourage you. There is precious
instruction to be got by finding we were wrong.
Let a man try faithfully, manfully, to be right;
he will grow daily more and more right.

THOMAS CARLYLE

By learning you will teach;
by teaching you will learn.

LATIN PROVERB

Timely Advice

Advice is like snow; the softer it falls
the longer it dwells upon, and the deeper
it sinks into the mind.

SAMUEL TAYLOR COLERIDGE

Get advice if you want your plans to work.
If you go to war, get the advice of others.

PROVERBS 20:18 NCV

All that is required to build a stable
relationship is the desire to do so...with
a little advice and counsel. Ultimately,
of course, we will rely on the principles
endorsed by the creator of families Himself.
That is pretty safe counsel.

JAMES DOBSON

Folly delights a man who lacks judgment,
but a man of understanding
keeps a straight course.
Plans fail for lack of counsel,
but with many advisers they succeed.
A man finds joy in giving an apt reply—
and how good is a timely word!

PROVERBS 15:21–23 NIV

Take the advice of a faithful friend,
and submit thy inventions to his censure.

THOMAS FULLER

Tell your friend a lie. If he keeps it secret,
then tell him the truth.

PORTUGUESE PROVERB

Humble in His Sight

As we enter more and more deeply into this
experience of being humbled and exalted, our
knowledge of God increases, and with it our
peace, our strength, and our joy. God help us,
then, to put our knowledge about God to this use,
that we all may in truth "know the Lord."

J. I. PACKER

The fear of the LORD teaches a man wisdom,
and humility comes before honor.

PROVERBS 15:33 NIV

Teach me, O Lord, to do Your will;
teach me to live worthily and humbly
in Your sight; for You are my Wisdom.

THOMAS À KEMPIS

All the ways of a man are pure in his own eyes,
but the LORD weighs the spirit.
Commit your work to the LORD,
and your plans will be established.
The LORD has made everything for its purpose,
even the wicked for the day of trouble.

PROVERBS 16:2–4 ESV

[The] first beatitude has nothing to do with
being materially destitute or financially bankrupt.
Jesus is placing value on a humble spirit,
on those who acknowledge a spiritual bankruptcy
in and of themselves. Where there is an absence
of well-polished pride and personal conceit, there
is a wholesome dependence on the living God.

CHARLES R. SWINDOLL

Well Done

There is much satisfaction in work well done; praise
is sweet, but there can be no happiness equal to the
joy of finding a heart that understands.

VICTOR ROBINSON

The gossip of bad people gets them in trouble;
the conversation of good people keeps them out of it.
Well-spoken words bring satisfaction;
well-done work has its own reward.

PROVERBS 12:13–14 MSG

I would give more for the private esteem and love
of one than for the public praise of ten thousand.

W. E. ALGER

Good friend, don't forget all I've taught you; take to heart my commands. They'll help you live a long, long time, a long life lived full and well.

PROVERBS 3:1–2 MSG

Let us begin from this moment to acknowledge Him in all our ways, and do everything, whatsoever we do, as service to Him and for His glory, depending upon Him alone for wisdom, and strength, and sweetness, and patience.

HANNAH WHITALL SMITH

Do well the little things now; so shall great things come to thee by and by asking to be done.

PERSIAN PROVERB

Inside Righteousness

Righteousness alone brings lasting peace.

THELMA GRAY

The mouth of the righteous is a fountain of life,
but the mouth of the wicked conceals violence.
Hatred stirs up strife, but love covers all offenses.

PROVERBS 10:11–12 ESV

The needed change within us is God's work,
not ours. The demand is for an inside job,
and only God can work from the inside.
We cannot attain or earn this righteousness
of the kingdom of God: it is a grace that is given.

RICHARD J. FOSTER

Peace within makes beauty without.

ENGLISH PROVERB

He who sows righteousness reaps a sure reward.... The wicked will not go unpunished, but those who are righteous will go free.

PROVERBS 11:18, 21 NIV

If there is righteousness in the heart, there will be beauty in the character. If there is beauty in the character, there will be harmony in the home. If there is harmony in the home, there will be order in the nation. When there is order in the nation, there will be peace in the world.

CHINESE PROVERB

The Gift of Friends

A word of encouragement to those we meet,
a cheerful smile in the supermarket, a card or
letter to a friend, a readiness to witness when
opportunity is given—all are practical ways in
which we may let His light shine through us.

ELIZABETH B. JONES

A cheerful look brings joy to the heart;
good news makes for good health.

PROVERBS 15:30 NLT

Your wealth is where your friends are.

LATIN PROVERB

Friendship is meeting another's
needs in a practical way.

BEVERLY LaHAYE

Many curry favor with a ruler, and everyone
is the friend of a man who gives gifts.

PROVERBS 19:6 NIV

Concrete reasons for loving another human
being not only need to be expressed to that
person, but will also help the person who
is doing the verbalizing. Dwelling in one's
mind on logical reasons for love does not
diminish the feelings of love, but increases them.

EDITH SCHAEFFER

A man's wisdom gives him patience;
it is to his glory to overlook an offense.

PROVERBS 19:11 NIV

A faithful friend is an image of God.

FRENCH PROVERB

True Understanding

For the LORD gives wisdom, and from his mouth come knowledge and understanding. He holds victory in store for the upright, he is a shield to those whose walk is blameless, for he guards the course of the just and protects the way of his faithful ones.

PROVERBS 2:6–8 NIV

It is never enough to know about spiritual things with your mind. Mental knowledge is not the same thing as truly understanding from the center of your being, which results from experiencing and doing.

TERESA OF AVILA

To understand and to be understood
makes our happiness on earth.

GERMAN PROVERB

Joyful is the person who finds wisdom,
the one who gains understanding.
For wisdom is more profitable than silver,
and her wages are better than gold.

PROVERBS 3:13–14 NLT

I abide in Christ and in doing so I find
rest, and the peace of God which passes all
understanding fills my heart and life.

JOHN HUNTER

Keep to God's Path

Listen...and be wise, and keep your
heart on the right path.

PROVERBS 23:19 NIV

Make no little plans; they have no magic to stir
men's blood and probably themselves will not
be realized. Make big plans; aim high in hope
and work, remembering that a noble, logical
diagram once recorded will not die.

DANIEL H. BURNHAM

In his heart a man plans his course,
but the LORD determines his steps.

PROVERBS 16:9 NIV

They are well guided that God guides.

SCOTTISH PROVERB

God's wisdom is always available to help
us choose from alternatives we face,
and help us to follow His eternal plan for us.

GLORIA GAITHER

God goes to those who come to Him.

RUSSIAN PROVERB

The very steps we take come from GOD;
otherwise how would we know where we're going?

PROVERBS 20:24 MSG

Whoever walks toward God one step,
God runs toward him two.

JEWISH PROVERB

Sharpen Your Character

Courage is what it takes to stand up and speak;
courage is also what it takes to sit down and listen.

WINSTON CHURCHILL

Speak up for those who cannot speak for
themselves, for the rights of all who are destitute.

PROVERBS 31:8 NIV

The firmest friendships have been formed
in mutual adversity; as iron is most strongly
united by the fiercest flame.

CHARLES C. COLTON

A man of character is a man of wealth.

EGYPTIAN PROVERB

A gem cannot be polished without friction,
nor a person perfected without adversity.

CHINESE PROVERB

*As iron sharpens iron, so a friend sharpens
a friend. As workers who tend a fig tree are
allowed to eat the fruit, so workers who protect
their employer's interests will be rewarded.*

PROVERBS 27:16–17 NLT

A good friend will sharpen your character,
draw your soul into the light, and challenge
your heart to love in a greater way.

Worry No More

An anxious heart weighs a man down,
but a kind word cheers him up.

PROVERBS 12:25 NIV

You can learn to overcome the worry of
anticipation. After you begin to experience
more and more the ready success of divine grace
upon all occasions, you will not worry about
things before they happen. When the time
comes for you to do your duty, you will find
God as in a clear mirror, and He will empower
you and make you fit to fulfill your obligations.

BROTHER LAWRENCE

When God gives hard bread
he gives sharp teeth.

GERMAN PROVERB

Since the house is on fire
let us warm ourselves.

ITALIAN PROVERB

A wise gardener plants his seeds, then
has the good sense not to dig them
up every few days to see if a crop is
on the way. Likewise, we must be
patient as God brings the answers...
in His own good time.

QUIN SHERRER

*Just as water mirrors your face,
so your face mirrors your heart.*

PROVERBS 27:19 MSG

Eternal Safety

God's Word acts as a light for our paths. It can
help scare off unwanted thoughts in our minds
and protect us from the enemy.

GARY SMALLEY AND JOHN TRENT

For the simple are killed by their turning away,
and the complacency of fools destroys them;
but whoever listens to me will dwell secure
and will be at ease, without dread of disaster.

PROVERBS 1:32–33 ESV

We shall steer safely through every storm, so long
as our heart is right, our intention fervent, our
courage steadfast, and our trust fixed on God.

FRANCIS DE SALES

Those who live in the Lord never
see each other for the last time.

GERMAN PROVERB

The fear of the LORD is a fountain of life,
turning a man from the snares of death.

PROVERBS 14:27 NIV

With God, life is eternal—both in quality
and length. There is no joy comparable
to the joy of discovering something
new from God, about God. If the
continuing life is a life of joy, we will
go on discovering, learning.

EUGENIA PRICE

God Is My Wisdom

Teach me, O Lord, to do Your will;
teach me to live worthily
and humbly in Your sight;
for You are my Wisdom,
who knew me truly, and who knew
me beforethe world was made,
and before I had my being.

THOMAS À KEMPIS

Whenever we build our lives on values
and principles that contradict the
time-honored wisdom of God's Word,
we are laying a foundation on the sand.

JAMES DOBSON

If you accept my words
and store up my commands within you,
turning your ear to wisdom
and applying your heart to understanding,
and if you call out for insight
and cry aloud for understanding,
and if you look for it as for silver
and search for it as for hidden treasure,
then you will understand the fear of the LORD
and find the knowledge of God.

PROVERBS 2:1–5 NIV

A person who doesn't know but knows that he
doesn't know is a student; teach him. A person
who knows but who doesn't know that he knows is
asleep; awaken him. But a person who knows and
knows that he knows is wise; follow him.

ASIAN PROVERB

Good Understanding

Obey my commands and live!
Guard my instructions as you guard your own eyes.
Tie them on your fingers as a reminder.
Write them deep within your heart.
Love wisdom like a sister;
make insight a beloved member of your family.

PROVERBS 7:2–4 NLT

A conflict cannot be entered with
the idea that one must "win."
There is no winning or losing
in a good conflict,
but a breaking through to better
understanding of each other.

CAROLE MAYHALL

Great thoughts always come from the heart.

FRENCH PROVERB

Communication is the meeting of meaning. When your meaning meets my meaning across the bridge of words, tones, acts, and deeds, when understanding occurs, then we know that we have communicated.

DAVID AUGSBURGER

The journey of a thousand miles starts with a single step.

CHINESE PROVERB

Good understanding wins favor, but the way of the unfaithful is hard.

PROVERBS 13:15 NIV

A mother understands what a child does not say.

JEWISH PROVERB

What's Next?

Wisdom ofttimes consists of knowing
what to do next.

HERBERT HOOVER

How much better to get wisdom than gold,
and good judgment than silver!
The path of the virtuous leads away from evil;
whoever follows that path is safe.

PROVERBS 16:16–17 NLT

The art of being happy lies in the power of
extracting happiness from common things.

HENRY WARD BEECHER

Charity looks at the need, not at the cause.

GERMAN PROVERB

He who gets wisdom loves his own soul;
he who cherishes understanding prospers.

PROVERBS 19:8 NIV

Compassionate the mountains rise
Dim with the wistful dimness of old eyes
That, having looked on life time out of mind,
Know that the simple gift of being kind
Is greater than all wisdom of the wise.

DUBOSE HEYWARD

When you were born, you cried and the world
rejoiced. Live your life in such a manner that
when you die the world cries and you rejoice.

INDIAN PROVERB

Stay True

If we can but for a moment see our mate as God
does, our compassion and love and
understanding may be changed for a lifetime.
A new view of our mate can only be
accomplished as God gives it to us by His grace,
and that grace is tapped through prayer.

JAMES DOBSON

Look for the good, not the evil, in the conduct
of members of the family.

JEWISH PROVERB

Find a good spouse, you find a good life—
and even more: the favor of GOD!

PROVERBS 18:22 MSG

A joy that's shared is a joy made double.

ENGLISH PROVERB

Do you know the saying, "Drink from your own rain barrel, draw water from your own spring-fed well"? It's true. Otherwise, you may one day come home and find your barrel empty and your well polluted.

PROVERBS 5:15–16 MSG

So live that when your spouse says he/she is married to you, he/she will be boasting.

Works, and not words, are the proof of love.

SPANISH PROVERB

Silent Times

God walks with us.... He scoops us up
in His arms or simply sits with us in silent
strength until we cannot avoid the awesome
recognition that yes, even now, He is here.

GLORIA GAITHER

It is foolish to belittle one's neighbor;
a sensible person keeps quiet.

PROVERBS 11:12 NLT

True friendship thrives through media
Of touch and sight and speech,
But often in the silent times
It most extends its reach.

CRAIG E. SATHOFF

To those who find themselves devoid of the presence of God, I would offer this counsel: wait on God. Wait, silent and still. Wait, attentive and responsive. Learn that trust precedes faith.

RICHARD J. FOSTER

A truly wise person uses few words;
a person with understanding is even-tempered.
Even fools are thought wise when they keep silent;
with their mouths shut, they seem intelligent.

PROVERBS 17:27–28 NLT

A friend is one who joyfully sings with you when you are on the mountain top, and silently walks beside you through the valley.

WILLIAM A. WARD

Honest Integrity

Confidence in others' honesty is no light
testimony to one's own integrity.

MICHEL DE MONTAIGNE

The way of the LORD is a stronghold
to those with integrity,
but it destroys the wicked.
The godly will never be disturbed,
but the wicked will be removed from the land.
The mouth of the godly person gives wise advice,
but the tongue that deceives will be cut off.
The lips of the godly speak helpful words,
but the mouth of the wicked
speaks perverse words.

PROVERBS 10:29–32 NLT

When one helps another, both are strong.

GERMAN PROVERB

Personal perfection is impossible,
but it is possible to aim for genuineness,
honesty, consistency, and moral purity,
and to frankly acknowledge it when we fail.

SUSAN ALEXANDER YATES

*Don't for a minute envy careless rebels;
soak yourself in the Fear-of-GOD—
That's where your future lies.
Then you won't be left with
an armload of nothing.*

PROVERBS 23:17–18 MSG

Power to Do Good

If you can help anybody even a little, be glad;
up the steps of usefulness and kindness,
God will lead you on to happiness and friendship.

MALTBIE D. BABCOCK

Do not withhold good from those who deserve
it when it's in your power to help them.

PROVERBS 3:27 NLT

Do not forget little kindnesses,
and do not remember small faults.

CHINESE PROVERB

Encouragement is being a good listener,
being positive, letting others know you
accept them for who they are.
It is offering hope, caring about
the feelings of another, understanding.

GIGI GRAHAM TCHIVIDJIAN

*A good person gives life to others;
the wise person teaches others how to live.*

PROVERBS 11:30 NCV

Loving Correction

Discipline your children,
and they will give you peace of mind
and will make your heart glad.

PROVERBS 29:17 NLT

Heavenly Father,
Teach me how to properly and fairly
discipline my children,
so that I may bring them to an understanding
of Your authority in their lives.
As they grow older, may the guidelines and
principles I have taught them lead
them to a life of self-control
based on following Your commandments. Amen.

KIM BOYCE

Praise the children and they will blossom.

IRISH PROVERB

*Do not reject the Lord's discipline,
and don't get angry when he corrects you.
The LORD corrects those he loves,
just as parents correct the child they delight in.*

PROVERBS 3:11–12 NCV

Disciplined people have learned the art of getting
up, dusting themselves off and starting over.

NEVA COYLE

An ounce of mother is worth a pound of clergy.

SPANISH PROVERB

Safe and Secure

When you lie down, you won't be afraid;
when you lie down, you will sleep in peace.

PROVERBS 3:24 NCV

May the God of love and peace set your heart
at rest and speed you on your journey. May He
meanwhile shelter you from disturbance by others
in the place of complete plenitude where you
will repose for ever in the vision of peace,
in the security of trust and in the restful
enjoyment of His riches.

RAYMOND OF PENYAFORT

Prayer is a long-term investment, one that will increase your sense of security because God is your protector. Keep at it every day, for prayer is the key of the day and the bolt of the evening. God is waiting to hear from you.

BARBARA JOHNSON

Those who respect the Lord will have security, and their children will be protected.

PROVERBS 14:26 NCV

Jesus Christ is no security against storms, but He is perfect security in storms. He has never promised you an easy passage, only a safe landing.

L. B. COWMAN

Look With Love

God looks at the world through the eyes of
love. If we, therefore, as human beings made
in the image of God, also want to see reality
rationally, that is, as it truly is, then we, too,
must learn to look at what we see with love.

ROBERTA BONDI

Friendship is love with understanding.

ANCIENT PROVERB

You will find as you look back upon
your life, that the moments when you
have really lived are the moments when you
have done things in the spirit of love.

HENRY DRUMMOND

I love those who love me,
And those who seek me diligently will find me.
Riches and honor are with me,
Enduring riches and righteousness.
My fruit is better than gold, yes, than fine gold,
And my revenue than choice silver.
I traverse the way of righteousness,
In the midst of the paths of justice,
That I may cause those who love me
to inherit wealth,
That I may fill their treasuries.

PROVERBS 8:17–21 NKJV

God works in moments.

FRENCH PROVERB

Written on My Heart

If God exists and we are made in His image
we can have real meaning, and we can
have real knowledge through what He has
communicated to us.

FRANCIS SCHAEFFER

Hold on to instruction, do not let it go;
guard it well, for it is your life.

PROVERBS 4:13 NIV

What keeps the Christian going...is the
knowledge of God written on his or her heart.

LINDA CLARK

There is deceit in the hearts of those who plot
evil, but joy for those who promote peace.

PROVERBS 12:20 NIV

Apply your heart to instruction
and your ears to words of knowledge.

PROVERBS 23:12 NIV

God is constantly taking knowledge of me in love,
and watching over me for my good.

J. I. PACKER

Hope deferred makes the heart sick, but a longing
fulfilled is a tree of life.

PROVERBS 13:12

Keep a green tree in your heart and perhaps
the singing bird will come.

CHINESE PROVERB

What Can I Give?

What can I give Him
Poor as I am?
If I were a shepherd,
I would give Him a lamb,
If I were a Wise Man,
I would do my part,—
But what I can I give Him,
Give my heart.

CHRISTINA ROSSETTI

He who is kind to the poor lends to the LORD,
and he will reward him for what he has done.

PROVERBS 19:17 NIV

Who gives to me, teaches me to give.

DUTCH PROVERB

A happy heart is the best service
we can give to God.

MARIE CHAPIAN

*The wise in heart are called discerning,
and pleasant words promote instruction.*

PROVERBS 16:21 NIV

As God loveth a cheerful giver,
so He also loveth a cheerful taker,
who takes hold on his gifts with a glad heart.

JOHN DONNE

Honest Words

Good leaders cultivate honest speech;
they love advisors who tell them the truth.

PROVERBS 16:13 MSG

As light is pleasant to the eye,
so is truth to the understanding.

RICHARD PELHAM

An honest answer is like
a kiss on the lips.

PROVERBS 24:26 NIV

When you grow up in an environment where…
commitment and dedication is not just talked
about but lived so fully, so honestly, there is no
way that it does not take root in your being.

YOLANDA KING

God be in my mouth,
And in my speaking;
God be in my heart,
And in my thinking.

BILLY GRAHAM

A wise man's heart guides his mouth,
and his lips promote instruction.

PROVERBS 16:23 NIV

There is nourishment from being encouraged
and held up by others when we are weak.
We are nourished from feedback from friends
whom we trust and who will be honest with us.

RICH BUHLER

Work Diligently

Lazy people don't even cook the game they catch,
but the diligent make use of everything they find.

PROVERBS 12:27 NLT

Learning is not attained by chance,
it must be sought for with ardor
and attended to with diligence.

ABIGAIL ADAMS

The opportunity that God sends does
not wake up one who is asleep.

SENEGALESE PROVERB

Thank God every morning when you get up that you have something to do that day which must be done, whether you like it or not. Being forced to work, and forced to do your best, will breed in you temperance and self-control, diligence and strength of will, cheerfulness and contentment, and a hundred virtues which the idle never know.

CHARLES KINGSLEY

The person who says it cannot be done should not interrupt the person doing it.

CHINESE PROVERB

The plans of the diligent lead to profit as surely as haste leads to poverty.

PROVERBS 21:5 NIV

Pray with Conviction

The LORD approves of those who are good,
but he condemns those who plan wickedness.

PROVERBS 12:2 NLT

How vital that we pray, armed with the knowledge
that God is in heaven. Pray with any lesser
conviction and your prayers are timid, shallow,
and hollow. But spend some time walking in the
workshop of the heavens, seeing what God has
done, and watch how your prayers are energized.

MAX LUCADO

Keep praying, but be thankful that God's
answers are wiser than your prayers!

WILLIAM CULBERTSON

A faithful man will abound with
blessings, but whoever hastens
to be rich will not go unpunished.

PROVERBS 28:20 ESV

When you pray, move your feet.

AFRICAN PROVERB

*The heart of the righteous ponders
how to answer,
but the mouth of the wicked
pours out evil things.
The LORD is far from the wicked
but he hears the prayer of the righteous.*

PROVERBS 15:28–29 ESV

Discerning the Holy

The discerning sets his face toward wisdom,
but the eyes of a fool are on the ends of the earth.

PROVERBS 17:24 ESV

God wants us to be present where we are.
He invites us to see and to hear what
is around us and, through it all,
to discern the footprints of the Holy.

RICHARD J. FOSTER

Rich people may think they are wise,
but a poor person with discernment
can see right through them.

PROVERBS 28:11

God often calls us to do things that we
do not have the ability to do. Spiritual
discernment is knowing if God calls you
to do something, God empowers you to do it.

SUZANNE FARNHAM

The heart of the discerning acquires knowledge;
the ears of the wise seek it out.

PROVERBS 18:15 NIV

To acquire knowledge, one must study;
but to acquire wisdom, one must observe.

MARILYN VOS SAVANT

Loyal Friends

Reliable friends who do what they say
are like cool drinks in sweltering heat—refreshing!
Like billowing clouds that bring no rain
is the person who talks big but never produces.

PROVERBS 25:13–14 MSG

Let not the grass grow on the path of friendship.

NATIVE AMERICAN PROVERB

A true friend is distinguished in the crisis
of hazard and necessity; when the gallantry
of his aid may show the worth
of his soul and the loyalty of his heart.

QUINTUS ENNIUS

The friends of my friends are my friends.

FRENCH PROVERB

Talk not of wasted affection!
Affection never was wasted;
If it enrich not the heart of another,
its water, returning
Back to their springs, like the rain,
shall fill them full of refreshment:
That which the fountain sends forth
returns again to the fountain.

LONGFELLOW

*An unreliable messenger stumbles into trouble,
but a reliable messenger brings healing.*

PROVERBS 13:17 NLT

Wisdom and Understanding

All [God's] glory and beauty come from within,
and there He delights to dwell.
His visits there are frequent,
His conversation sweet,
His comforts refreshing,
His peace passing all understanding.

THOMAS À KEMPIS

Buy the truth, and do not sell it,
Also wisdom and instruction and understanding.

PROVERBS 23:23 NKJV

A fool finds pleasure in evil conduct,
but a man of understanding delights in wisdom.

PROVERBS 10:23 NIV

Wise people store up knowledge,
But the mouth of the foolish is near destruction.

PROVERBS 10:14 NKJV

Knowledge is proud that it knows so much;
wisdom is humble that it knows no more.

WILLIAM COWPER

*A patient man has great understanding,
but a quick-tempered man displays folly.*

PROVERBS 14:29 NIV

If you know the father and grandfather
you may trust the son.

MOROCCAN PROVERB

Treasure Justice

When justice is done, it brings joy
to the righteous but terror to evildoers.

PROVERBS 21:15 NIV

His justice is full and complete,
His mercy to us has no end;
the clouds are a path for His feet,
He comes on the wings of the wind.

CHRISTOPHER IDLE

Evil people do not understand justice, but those
who follow the Lord understand it completely.

PROVERBS 28:5 NCV

If a child lives with fairness, he learns justice.

DOROTHY LAW NOLTE

You can find me on Righteous Road—
that's where I walk—
at the intersection of Justice Avenue,
Handing out life to those who love me,
filling their arms with life—armloads of life!

PROVERBS 8:20–21 MSG

Justice and power must be brought together,
so that whatever is just may be powerful,
and whatever is powerful may be just.

BLAISE PASCAL

Beautiful Disposition

Happiness is in great measure the result of
our own dispositions and actions.

HANNAH WEBSTER FOSTER

If you prize wisdom, she will make you great.
Embrace her, and she will honor you.
She will place a lovely wreath on your head;
she will present you with a beautiful crown.

PROVERBS 4:8–9 NLT

I have learned from experience that the greater
part of our happiness or misery depends on our
dispositions and not on our circumstances.

MARTHA WASHINGTON

A misty morning does not signify a cloudy day.

ANCIENT PROVERB

A cheerful disposition
is good for your health;
gloom and doom leave you bone-tired.

PROVERBS 17:22 MSG

We were made for God. Only by being in some
respect like Him, only by being a manifestation of
His beauty, lovingkindness, wisdom, or goodness,
has any earthly beloved excited our love.

C. S. LEWIS

The glory is not in never failing,
but in rising every time you fail.

CHINESE PROVERB

Deeper Understanding

The purposes of a man's heart are deep waters,
but a man of understanding draws them out.

PROVERBS 20:5 NIV

Reflection...enables our minds to be stretched in
three different directions—the direction that leads
to a proper relationship with God, the relationship
that leads to a healthy relationship with others,
and the relationship that leads to a deeper
understanding of oneself.

MARK CONNOLLY

A truly wise person uses few words;
a person with understanding is even-tempered.

PROVERBS 17:27 NLT

No beard, no understanding.

It might be a good idea to ask ourselves how we develop our capacity to choose for joy. Maybe we could spend a moment at the end of each day and decide to remember that day—whatever may have happened—as a day to be grateful for. In so doing we increase our heart's capacity to choose joy.

Henri J. M. Nouwen

When a country is lawless, it has one ruler after another; but when it is led by a leader with understanding and knowledge, it continues strong.

Proverbs 28:2 ncv

The Joy of Righteousness

As we pray...God is inviting us deeper in and higher up. There is training in righteousness, transforming power, new joy, deeper intimacy.

RICHARD J. FOSTER

Wealth is worthless in the day of wrath, but
righteousness delivers from death.
The righteousness of the blameless makes
a straight way for them, but the wicked are
brought down by their own wickedness.
The righteousness of the upright delivers them,
but the unfaithful are trapped by evil desires.

PROVERBS 11:4–6 NIV

One joy scatters a hundred griefs.

CHINESE PROVERB

We are forgiven and righteous because of Christ's
sacrifice; therefore we are pleasing to God in spite
of our failures. Christ alone is the source of our
forgiveness, freedom, joy, and purpose.

ROBERT S. McGEE

*The LORD detests the sacrifice of the wicked,
but the prayer of the upright pleases him.
The LORD detests the way of the wicked
but he loves those who pursue righteousness.*

PROVERBS 15:8–9 NIV

There is no pillow so soft as a clear conscience.

FRENCH PROVERB

Virtuous Worker

When Jesus was on earth, it wasn't an accident
that He came as a blue-collar worker, nor
that His parables would deal with things like
sowing seed, vineyard laborers, harvesters, house
building, and swine tending. In Him there is
no hierarchy of importance vocationally, there's
only the wise use of the talents He dispenses.

LARRY KREIDER

Those who work their land will have plenty
of food, but the ones who chase empty
dreams instead will end up poor.

PROVERBS 28:19 NCV

When you are laboring for others let it be with
the same zeal as if it were for yourself.

CHINESE PROVERB

Do you see a man skilled in his work?
He will serve before kings;
he will not serve before obscure men.

PROVERBS 22:29 NIV

Wisdom is knowing what to do next,
skill is knowing how to do it,
and virtue is doing it.

DAVID STARR JORDAN

There are many virtuous and capable
women in the world,
but you surpass them all!

PROVERBS 31:29 NLT

Beauty without virtue is a flower
without perfume.

FRENCH PROVERB

Everyday Wisdom

The tongue of the wise uses knowledge rightly,
But the mouth of fools pours forth foolishness.

PROVERBS 15:2 NKJV

This voice that calls to us out of the everyday
moments of life is called the wisdom of God.
This wisdom is infused into nature
and the laws that govern her, and into
human nature and the laws that govern it.

KEN GIRE

I was like a child by his side.
I was delighted every day,
enjoying his presence all the time,
enjoying the whole world,
and delighted with all its people.

PROVERBS 8:30–31 NCV

The eyes are of little use if the mind be blind.

ARAB PROVERB

Wicked people are stubborn,
but good people think carefully
about what they do.
There is no wisdom, understanding,
or advice that can succeed against the Lord.

PROVERBS 21:29–30 NCV

God's will is determined by His wisdom
which always perceives,
and His goodness which always embraces
the intrinsically good.

C. S. LEWIS

Listen Closely

Pay attention to my words;
listen closely to what I say.
Don't ever forget my words;
keep them always in mind.
They are the key to life for those who find them;
they bring health to the whole body.
Be careful what you think,
because your thoughts run your life.

PROVERBS 4:20–23 NCV

A true friend is someone who listens to us with
real concentration and expresses sincere care for
our struggles and pains. She makes us feel that
something very deep is happening to us.

HELEN FEENEY

Look up at all the stars in the night sky
and hear your Father saying, "I carefully
set each one in its place. Know that
I love you more than these." Sit by the
lake's edge, listening to the water lapping
the shore and hear your Father gently
calling you to that place near His heart.

Give instruction to a wise man,
and he will be still wiser;
Teach a just man,
and he will increase in learning.

PROVERBS 9:9 NKJV

Pay attention to the small things—
the kite flies because of its tail.

HAWAIIAN PROVERB

You Will Receive Mercy

Have confidence in God's mercy,
for when you think He is a long way from you,
He is often quite near.

THOMAS À KEMPIS

If you hide your sins, you will not succeed.
If you confess and reject them,
you will receive mercy.

PROVERBS 28:13 NCV

No offense by another person could possibly
equal our guilt before God, yet He has
forgiven us; are we not obligated
to show the same mercy to others?

JAMES DOBSON

The best memory is that which forgets
nothing but injuries. Write kindness
in marble and write injuries in the dust.

PERSIAN PROVERB

Doing what is right makes a nation great,
but sin will bring disgrace to any people.

PROVERBS 14:34 NCV

We may think we want justice.
What we want is mercy. We need it.

B. C. FORBES

In mercy and truth
Atonement is provided for iniquity;
And by the fear of the LORD one departs from evil.

PROVERBS 16:6 NKJV

Share Love

The less we have, the more we give.
Seems absurd, but it's the logic of love.

MOTHER TERESA

A gift opens the way for the giver
and ushers him into the presence of the great.

PROVERBS 18:16 NIV

In all your growing and increasing godliness,
don't forget to love. Someone near you may
need a hug more than an insight.

NEVA COYLE

The hand that gives, gathers.

ENGLISH PROVERB

In the morning let our hearts gaze upon
God's love and the love He has allowed
us to share, and in the beauty of that vision,
let us go forth to meet the day.

ROY LESSIN

The cheerful of heart has a continual feast.
Better is a little with the fear of the LORD
than great treasure and trouble with it.

PROVERBS 15:15–16 ESV

He made you so you could share in His creation,
could love and laugh and know Him.

TED GRIFFEN

Gratitude is the heart's memory.

FRENCH PROVERB

The Blessing of Generations

The mark of a good father is his
compassionate understanding of the fact
that mistakes are a part of growing up.

GARY SMALLEY AND JOHN TRENT

Train a child in the way he should go,
and when he is old he will not turn from it.

PROVERBS 22:6 NIV

Father, help me to take the time to create
stories with my children. May good memories
hold the generations together.

SCOTT WALKER

Children are a bridge to heaven.

PERSIAN PROVERB

In youth acquire that which may requite
you for the deprivations of old age; and if
you are mindful that old age has wisdom for
its food, you will so exert yourself in youth,
that your old age will not lack sustenance.

LEONARDO DA VINCI

The glory of young men is their strength,
gray hair the splendor of the old.

PROVERBS 20:29 NIV

Where can one better be than
the bosom of one's own family.

FRENCH PROVERB

Find Your Path

God can help me clear away the obstructions
and see clearly where the path is.

GLORIA GAITHER

The path of life leads upward for the wise;
they leave the grave behind.

PROVERBS 15:24 NLT

Look back from where we have come.
The path was at times an open road of joy,
At others a steep and bitter track of stones
and pain. How could we know the joy
without the suffering? And how could we
endure the suffering but that we are warmed
and carried on the breast of God?

DESMOND M. TUTU

For a man's ways are in full view of the LORD,
and he examines all his paths.

PROVERBS 5:21 NIV

What we need is not new light,
but new sight; not new paths,
but new strength to walk in the old ones;
not new duties but new wisdom from
on High to fulfill those that are plain before us.

*Don't turn off the road of goodness;
keep away from evil paths.*

PROVERBS 4:27 NCV

Love Your Enemies

Love is the only force capable
of transforming an enemy into a friend.

MARTIN LUTHER KING JR.

If your enemy is hungry, give him food to eat;
if he is thirsty, give him water to drink.
In doing this, you will heap burning coals
on his head, and the LORD will reward you.

PROVERBS 25:21–22 NIV

If we refuse to treat people as our enemies,
we have the best possible chance
of winning them to be our friends.

CATHERINE GORE

When a man's ways are pleasing to the LORD,
he makes even his enemies live at peace with him.

PROVERBS 16:7 NIV

The best to give:
to your enemy is forgiveness;
to an opponent, tolerance;
to a friend, your heart.

LORD BALFOUR

Don't be happy when your enemy is defeated;
don't be glad when he is overwhelmed

PROVERBS 24:17 NCV

He who forgives ends the quarrel.

AFRICAN PROVERB

Patience and Diligence

If your determination is fixed, I do not counsel
you to despair. Few things are impossible
to diligence and skill. Great works are performed
not by strength, but perseverance.

SAMUEL JOHNSON

Patience is better than strength. Controlling
your temper is better than capturing a city.

PROVERBS 16:32 NCV

Patience and diligence, like faith,
remove mountains.

WILLIAM PENN

The soul of the sluggard craves and gets nothing,
while the soul of the diligent is richly supplied.

PROVERBS 13:4 ESV

With patience a ruler may be persuaded,
and a soft tongue will break a bone.

PROVERBS 25:15 ESV

Have patience with all things, but chiefly
have patience with yourself. Do not lose
courage in considering your own imperfections
but instantly set about remedying them—
every day begin the task anew.

FRANCIS DE SALES

Diligent hands will rule,
but laziness ends in slave labor.

PROVERBS 12:24 NIV

Nothing teaches patience like a garden.
You may go round and watch the opening bud
from day to day, but it takes its own time.

MENNONITE WRITING

Guard Instruction

He who obeys instructions guards his life, but he
who is contemptuous of his ways will die.

PROVERBS 19:16 NIV

You can trust the Lord too little,
but you can never trust Him too much.

He who heeds the word wisely will find good,
And whoever trusts in the Lord, happy is he.

PROVERBS 16:20 NKJV

Neither let mistakes nor wrong directions,
of which every man, in his studies and elsewhere,
falls into many, discourage you. There is precious
instruction to be got by finding we were wrong.

THOMAS CARLYLE

Listen to advice and accept instruction,
and in the end you will be wise.

PROVERBS 19:20 NIV

*The Lord's Prayer is a floor plan of the
house of God: a step-by-step description
of how God meets our needs when we
dwell in Him. Everything that occurs in
a healthy house is described in this prayer.
Protection, instruction, forgiveness,
provision...all occur under God's roof.*

MAX LUCADO

I am teaching you true and reliable
words so that you can give true answers
to anyone who asks.

PROVERBS 22:21 NCV

Divine Ownership

Honor the LORD with your possessions,
And with the firstfruits of all your increase;
So your barns will be filled with plenty,
And your vats will overflow with new wine.

PROVERBS 3:9–10 NKJV

Know your sheep by name;
carefully attend to your flocks;
(Don't take them for granted;
possessions don't last forever, you know.)
And then, when the crops are in
and the harvest is stored in the barns,
You can knit sweaters from lambs' wool,
and sell your goats for a profit;
There will be plenty of milk and meat
to last your family through the winter.

PROVERBS 27:23–27 MSG

I am happy in having learned to distinguish
between ownership and possession. Books,
pictures, and all the beauty of the world
belong to those who love and understand
them—not usually to those who possess
them. All of these things that I am entitled
to I have—I own them by divine right.
So I care not a bit who possesses them.

JAMES HOWARD KEHLER

Nobody robs a bank with everyone watching,
Yet that's what these people are doing—
they're doing themselves in.
When you grab all you can get,
that's what happens:
the more you get, the less you are.

PROVERBS 1:17–19 MSG

Live Generously

Give generously, save consistently,
and never spend more money than you have.

MARY HUNT

Generous hands are blessed hands
because they give bread to the poor.
Kick out the troublemakers and things
will quiet down; you need a break
from bickering and griping!

PROVERBS 22:9–10 MSG

The fountain of beauty is the heart,
and every generous thought
illustrates the walls of your chamber.

FRANCIS QUARLES

God shares with the person who is generous.

IRISH PROVERB

A generous man will prosper;
he who refreshes others will himself be refreshed.

PROVERBS 11:25 NIV

People who deal with life generously
and large-heartedly go on multiplying
relationships to the end.

ARTHUR CHRISTOPHER BENSON

Whoever oppresses a poor man insults his Maker,
but he who is generous to the needy honors him.

PROVERBS 14:31 ESV

Flowers leave their fragrance
on the hand that bestows them.

CHINESE PROVERB

Search Me, O Lord

The lamp of the LORD searches the spirit
of a man; it searches out his inmost being.

PROVERBS 20:27 NIV

Only God gives true peace—a quiet gift
He sets within us just when we think we've
exhausted our search for it.

It is the glory of God to conceal things,
but the glory of kings is to search things out.

PROVERBS 25:2 ESV

The treasure our heart searches for is found
in the ocean of God's love.

JANET L. WEAVER SMITH

I have since learned that when a baffling or painful experience comes, the crucial thing is not always to find the right answers, but to ask the right questions. Self-questioning is a far more essential ingredient in life that I ever supposed. It's the water that keeps the modeling clay of our life from hardening into something forever rigid and unchanging. To refuse to ask honest questions of ourselves ultimately means shutting ourselves off from revelation. Often it is simply the right question at the right time that propels us on into the journey of awakening.

SUE MONK KIDD

Filled with Grace

First, help me never to tell a lie.
Second, give me neither poverty nor riches!
Give me just enough to satisfy my needs.

PROVERBS 30:8 NLT

In the beginning, as we are learning to pray,
our will is in a struggle with God's will.
In time, however, we begin to enter into
a grace-filled releasing of our will and
a flowing into the will of the Father.

RICHARD J. FOSTER

My child, listen to your father's teaching
and do not forget your mother's advice.
Their teaching will be like flowers in your hair
or a necklace around your neck.

PROVERBS 1:8–9 NCV

*An evil man is ensnared
in his transgression,
but a righteous man sings
and rejoices.
A righteous man knows
the rights of the poor;
a wicked man does not understand
such knowledge.*

PROVERBS 29:6–7 ESV

The grace of God is equal to...the most
unfavorable circumstances. Its glory is to
transform a curse into blessing and show to men
and angels of ages yet to come that where sin
abounded, grace did much more abound.

A. B. SIMPSON

Rejoice in Your Family

There is no more liberating experience than the
joy of loving one's spouse and children,
the confidence of being loved,
and the knowledge that such love can move
mountains and make nations whole.

GARY BAUER

Be wise, my son, and bring joy to my heart; then I
can answer anyone who treats me with contempt.

PROVERBS 27:11 NIV

Biblical principles offer the most healthy
approach to family living—even turning
stress to our advantage.

JAMES DOBSON

It is easier to rule a kingdom
than to regulate a family.

JAPANESE PROVERB

A happy family is but an earlier heaven.

SIR JOHN BOWRING

Parents rejoice when their children turn out well;
wise children become proud parents. So make
your father happy! Make your mother proud!

PROVERBS 23:24–25 MSG

Children are poor men's riches.

ENGLISH PROVERB

In the midst of the praying, it is comforting to
remember that God considers families important.
Before He called a nation, He created a family.

QUIN SHERRER

Wisdom Is Knowing

With God our trust
can be abandoned, utterly free.
In Him are no limitations,
no flaws, no weaknesses.
His judgment is perfect,
His knowledge of us is perfect,
His love is perfect.
God alone is trustworthy.

Eugenia Price

When they cry for help, I will not answer.
Though they anxiously search for me,
they will not find me.
For they hated knowledge
and chose not to fear the Lord.
They rejected my advice
and paid no attention when I corrected them.

Proverbs 1:28–30 nlt

It takes wisdom to have a good family,
and it takes understanding to make it strong.

PROVERBS 24:3 NCV

Knowledge is knowing a fact.
Wisdom is knowing
what to do with that fact.

*Know also that wisdom is sweet to your soul;
if you find it, there is a future hope for you,
and your hope will not be cut off.*

PROVERBS 24:14 NIV

Seize opportunity by the beard,
for it is bald behind.

BULGARIAN PROVERB

The Lord's Purpose

The awe that we sense or ought
to sense when standing
in the presence of a human being
is a moment of intuition
for the likeness of God which
is concealed in his essence.

ABRAHAM JOSHUA HESCHEL

God has a purpose for your life
and no one else can take your place.

God possesses infinite knowledge and an
awareness which is uniquely His. At all times,
even in the midst of any type of suffering,
I can realize that He knows, loves, watches,
understands, and more than that,
He has a purpose.

BILLY GRAHAM

*Many are the plans in the
mind of a man,
but it is the purpose of the LORD
that will stand.*

PROVERBS 19:21 ESV

There would be no sense in asking why if one
did not believe in anything. The word itself
presupposes purpose. Purpose presupposes a
powerful intelligence. Somebody has to have
been responsible. It is because we believe
in God that we address questions to Him.

ELISABETH ELLIOT

The mocker seeks wisdom and finds none,
but knowledge comes easily to the discerning.

PROVERBS 14:6 NIV

My Strong Tower

Do not take overmuch thought for
tomorrow. God, who has led you safely
on so far, will lead you on to the end.
Be altogether at rest in the loving holy
confidence which you ought to have
in His heavenly Providence.

FRANCIS DE SALES

Regardless of whether we feel strong or weak
in our faith, we remember that our assurance
is not based upon our ability to conjure up
some special feeling. Rather, it is built upon
a confident assurance in the faithfulness
of God. We focus on His trustworthiness
and especially on His steadfast love.

RICHARD J. FOSTER

The name of the LORD is a strong tower:
the righteous run to it and are safe.

PROVERBS 18:10 NIV

It is a good and safe rule to sojourn
in every place as if you meant to spend
your life there, never omitting
an opportunity of doing a kindness,
or speaking a true word, or making a friend.

JOHN RUSKIN

Their Defender is strong;
he will take up their case against you.

PROVERBS 23:11 NIV

Even the highest towers begin from the ground.

CHINESE PROVERB

The Beginning of Knowledge

What matters supremely is not the fact that
I know God, but the larger fact which
underlies it—the fact that He knows me.
I am graven on the palms of His hands.
I am never out of His mind. All my knowledge
of Him depends on His sustained initiative
in knowing me. I know Him because He first
knew me, and continues to know me.

J. I. PACKER

The fear of the LORD
is the beginning of knowledge,
but fools despise wisdom and discipline.

PROVERBS 1:7 NIV

The greatest honor we can give God is to live
gladly because of the knowledge of His love.

JULIAN OF NORWICH

God guards knowledge with a passion,
but he'll have nothing to do with deception.

PROVERBS 22:12 MSG

It's usually through our hard times, the unexpected
and not-according-to-plan times, that we
experience God in more intimate ways. We
discover an unquenchable longing to know Him
more. It's a passion that isn't concerned that life
fall within certain predictable lines, but a passion
that pursues God and knows He is relentless in
His pursuit of each one of us.

WENDY MOORE

A Word to the Wise

When words are many, sin is not absent,
but he who holds his tongue is wise.

PROVERBS 10:19 NIV

Rather than placing all the emphasis on earthly,
tangible treasures, our Lord instructs us to
turn our attention to those intangible treasures
that defy destruction and cannot be stolen—
eternal treasures that keep the perspective clear.

CHARLES R. SWINDOLL

Pay attention and listen to the sayings of the wise;
apply your heart to what I teach,
for it is pleasing when you keep them in your
heart and have all of them ready on your lips.

PROVERBS 22:17–18 NIV

Character is so largely affected by associations
that we cannot afford to be indifferent
as to who and what our friends are.
They write their names in our albums,
but they do more, they help make us what we are.
Be therefore careful in selecting them;
and when wisely selected, never sacrifice them.

M. HULBURD

A truthful witness gives honest testimony,
but a false witness tells lies.
Reckless words pierce like a sword,
but the tongue of the wise brings healing.
Truthful lips endure forever,
but a lying tongue lasts only a moment.

PROVERBS 12:17–19 NIV

Quietly Trust

If the Lord be with us, we have
no cause of fear. His eye is upon us, His arm
over us, His ear open to our prayer—His grace
sufficient, His promise unchangeable.

JOHN NEWTON

The fear of the LORD leads to life,
and whoever has it rests satisfied;
he will not be visited by harm.

PROVERBS 19:23 ESV

Lord, grant me a quiet mind,
That trusting Thee, for Thou art kind,
I may go on without a fear,
For Thou, my Lord, art always near.

AMY CARMICHAEL

The blessing of the LORD makes a person rich,
and he adds no sorrow with it.

PROVERBS 10:22 NLT

What steps of wisdom lead us to
a place of trust? Let us look for what
is good in our situation.
Minimize what is bad. Calmly,
quietly trust in God. Relax and let
God take full control. Yes, quietly trust.

THELMA MCMILLAN

It is in the shelter of each other that people live.

IRISH PROVERB

Fountain of Wisdom

The fear of the LORD is the beginning of wisdom,
and the knowledge of the Holy One is insight.

PROVERBS 9:10 ESV

By learning you will teach;
by teaching you will learn.

LATIN PROVERB

My children, listen when your father corrects you.
Pay attention and learn good judgment,
for I am giving you good guidance.
Don't turn away from my instructions.

PROVERBS 4:1–2 NLT

A kind heart is a fountain of gladness, making
everything in its vicinity freshen into smiles.

WASHINGTON IRVING

If we have been learning to worship
God and to trust Him, the crisis will reveal
that we will go to the breaking point and not
break in our confidence in Him.

OSWALD CHAMBERS

The light of the righteous shines brightly,
but the lamp of the wicked is snuffed out.

PROVERBS 13:9 NIV

You can teach a student a lesson for a day;
but if you can teach him to learn by creating
curiosity, he will continue the learning
process as long as he lives.

CLAY P. BEDFORD

An Invitation

If you have ever:

    questioned if this is all there is to life...

    wondered what happens when you die...

    felt a longing for purpose or significance...

    wrestled with resurfacing anger...

    struggled to forgive someone...

    known there is a "higher power" but couldn't define it...

    sensed you have a role to play in the world...

    experienced success and still felt empty afterward...

then consider Jesus.

A great teacher from two millennia ago, Jesus of Nazareth, freely chose to show our Maker's everlasting love for us by offering to take all of our flaws, darkness, and mistakes into His very body (1 Peter 2:24). The result was His death on a cross. But the story doesn't end there. God raised Him to newness of life, and invites us to believe this truth in our hearts and follow Jesus into eternal life.

If you confess with your mouth that Jesus is Lord and believe in your heart that God raised him from the dead, you will be saved. —ROMANS 10:9